NSPCC

TECHOSAURUS SAVES THE SCHOOL!

Published in the UK by Sweet Cherry Publishing Limited, 2025
Unit 36, Vulcan House, Vulcan Road,
Leicester LE5 3EF, United Kingdom

Unit 31, The Pottery, Bakers Point,
Pottery Road, Dún Laoghaire,
Dublin A96 EV18, Ireland

2 4 6 8 10 9 7 5 3 1

ISBN: 978-1-80263-736-6

Techosaurus Saves the School

Illustrations by Kevin Payne
Original characters designed by Jamie Nash

www.sweetcherrypublishing.com

Printed and bound in China

MIX
Paper | Supporting responsible forestry
FSC® C188448
FSC
www.fsc.org

Techosaurus and their friends at the
NSPCC would like to say a special thank you to
Albion Primary School, Southwark Park Primary School,
Rotherhithe Primary School, Canada Water Library,
Theatre Peckham and everyone whose kind
support helped us make this book.
We couldn't have done it without you.

Mrs Bronto's class of dinosaurs are very excited because today they are playing an online game.

I NEED YOUR HELP WITH A SPECIAL MISSION ... TO SAVE THE SCHOOL!

'Online dinobots have been trying to spoil our fun,' says Mrs Bronto. 'But together we can stop their online tricks.'

- **BE KIND** when you **PLAY** online.
- **PROTECT** your personal information, like your birthday and your passwords.
- **ASK** an adult before you do something new.
- **SAY** when something makes you feel uncomfortable.

‘Are you ready, dinos?’
asks Mrs Bronto.

Before the dinos can reply, they hear a loud

PING!

come from the class computer.

Techosaurus runs over to find a message on the screen.

But Friendosaurus is not on the school register.

They might not be who they say they are!

What should the dinos do? Press the correct button.

Techosaurus tells their friends not to reply.

WELL DONE, DINOS! YOU PROTECTED YOUR PERSONAL INFORMATION.
BEEP!
ROAR!
WE'LL TRICK YOU NEXT TIME, DINOS!

Mrs Bronto is proud of the little dinos.

She puts on a funny video as a treat.

ME-ME-ME! MEOOOOOOOW!

Suddenly, the screen turns dark ...

The video changes ...

A scary monster comes running towards them!

'I'm scared,'
says the littlest dino.
'What should we do?'

Techosaurus turns off
the screen so they can't
see the scary monster.

But what should
they do next?

Help Techosaurus decide what to do.

Press the correct button.

'Let's tell Mrs Bronto about the video,' says Techosaurus. 'She can help us.'

The dinos all stomp over to Mrs Bronto.

WELL DONE, DINOS!
YOU REMEMBERED TO SAY SOMETHING WHEN YOU SAW SOMETHING THAT MADE YOU FEEL UNCOMFORTABLE.
BEEP!
ROAR!
THEY'VE BEATEN US AGAIN!

'PLAY, PROTECT,

WE SAVED THE

ASK, SAY.

SCHOOL TODAY!'

After school, the dinos are playing at Techosaurus's house.

They video call Dinogran to show her their new dance routine.

Suddenly, the screen changes.

A scary film pops up next to Dinogran.

Techosaurus turns off the tablet so they can't see the scary video – but now they can't see Dinogran either!

Can you remember what the dinos need to do?

Press the correct button.

'We need to **SAY** something!' says Techosaurus.

'Let's tell Dinomum!'

Techosaurus marches to the garden, followed by their dino friends.

'What's the matter?' asks Dinomum.

Techosaurus tells her all about the scary video.

Dinomum gets rid of the scary video and calls Dinogran again.

'Now, let's get dancing again!'

says Dinomum.

The end.

HELP YOUR CHILD STAY SAFE ONLINE BY FOLLOWING THESE TOP TIPS:

PLAY:

The internet can be a lot of fun, but it's important to encourage your child to be kind online so that everyone else can have fun too! Lead by example, showing your child how to treat others with kindness and respect.

PROTECT:

Use app settings to help keep you and your child's personal information, photos and videos private. Use unique passwords to avoid others being able to access your information.